SPIRITUAL WISDOM

For

ENTREPRENEURS

Reaching Your Full Potential in Entrepreneurship

Companion Workbook

Dr. Patrick W. Sanders Sr.

This Workbook belongs to:

Name: _____

Phone: _____

VISION FOR MY BUSINESS

_____

_____

_____

_____

_____

_____

_____

_____

_____

_____

_____

_____

_____

_____

_____

_____

_____

_____

PERSONAL MISSION STATEMENT

_____

_____

_____

_____

_____

_____

_____

_____

_____

_____

_____

_____

_____

_____

_____

_____

_____

_____

_____

VISION FOR MY LIFE

_____

_____

_____

_____

_____

_____

_____

_____

_____

_____

_____

_____

_____

_____

_____

_____

_____

Please use this companion workbook to journal your thoughts as you read spiritual wisdom for entrepreneurs.

The Wisdom of Vision

"Good business leaders create a vision, articulate the vision, passionately own the vision, and relentlessly drive it to completion."- Jack Welch

Reflection Time

1. How do you define vision in your own life?

_____

_____

_____

_____

2. How can vision help you build your business and make you a successful entrepreneur?

_____

_____

_____

_____

3. Reflect on the times someone questioned your vision. How did you handle it? How would you handle it today?

_____

_____

_____

_____

_____

4. What is your plan to eliminate the white noise and naysayers in your life?

_____

_____

_____

_____

_____

THE WISDOM OF ANSWERING OF THE CALL

"God did not direct His call to Isaiah— Isaiah overheard God saying, '. . . who will go for Us?' The call of God is not just for a select few, but for everyone. Whether I hear God's call or not depends on the condition of my ears, and exactly what I hear depends upon my spiritual attitude."
- Oswald Chambers

Reflection Time

1. When did God call you? What are you called to do?

_____

_____

_____

_____

_____

2. What is your plan to execute the calling on your life?

_____

_____

_____

_____

_____

The Wisdom of Identity

"When I discover who I am, I'll be free."
— Ralph Ellison, Invisible Man

Reflection Time

1. What is your identity? Who are you?

_____

_____

_____

_____

_____

2. Ask 5 people close to you what your personal brand is. Compare their feedback to what you believe your own brand to be.

_____

_____

_____

_____

_____

The Wisdom of Giving

"I believe that we all have a responsibility to give back. No one becomes successful without lots of demanding work, support from others, and a little luck. Giving back creates a virtuous cycle that makes everyone more successful." — *Ron Conway*

Reflection Time

1. What do you feel your responsibility is as it relates to giving?

_____

_____

_____

_____

_____

2. Think of some charitable organizations that align with your personal and business goals. What can you do to get involved?

_____

_____

_____

_____

_____

The Wisdom of Collaboration/Community

"And let us consider how to stir up one another to love and good works, not neglecting to meet, as is the habit of some, but encouraging one another, and all the more as you see the Day drawing near." Hebrews 10:24-25

Reflection Time

1. Who have you collaborated with to achieve your business goals?

_____

_____

_____

_____

_____

2. What steps can I take to build community in my life?

_____

_____

_____

_____

_____

The Wisdom of Stewardship

"If God was the Owner, I was the manager. I needed to adopt a steward's mentality toward the assets He had entrusted – Not Given – to me. A steward manager's assets for the Owner's benefit. The steward carries no sense of entitlement to the assets he manages. It's his job to find out what the owner wants done with His assets, then carry out His will." – Randy Alcorn

Reflection Time

1. What do you see as your talents in business/personal life?

_____

_____

_____

_____

2. How can you use the resources you have been given more effectively?

_____

_____

_____

_____

The Wisdom of Preparation

"I believe success is preparation, because opportunity is going to knock on your door sooner or later, but are you prepared to answer that?" – Omar Epps

Reflection Time

1. How do you need to prepare yourself?

_____

_____

_____

_____

_____

2. What steps do you need to take to build a plan?

_____

_____

_____

_____

_____

The Wisdom of Failure

"If "Plan A" does not work, the alphabet has 25 more letters." --- Author Unknown

Reflection Time

1. What was your greatest failure?

_____

_____

_____

_____

_____

2. What can you do to mitigate future failure or bounce back after failure occurs?

_____

_____

_____

_____

_____

The Wisdom of Grit

"Grit is that extra something that separates the most successful people from the rest. It is passion, perseverance, and stamina that we must channel to stick with our dreams until they become a reality."
– Travis Bradberry

Reflection Time

1. Think of a time in your life where you used grit to get through?

_____

_____

_____

_____

_____

2. What does a fixed mindset mean to you?

_____

_____

_____

_____

_____

The Wisdom of the 2 R's

"This is a hard truth for some to accept: that a lack of resources may not be their true constraint, just a lack of resourcefulness." – David Burkus

"Resilience isn't a single skill. It's a variety of skills and coping mechanisms. To bounce back from bumps in the road as well as failures, you should focus on emphasizing the positive." – Jean Chatzky

Reflection Time

1. Who is the most resourceful person you know? How are they resourceful?

_____

_____

_____

_____

2. Who is the most resilient person you know? How are they resilient?

_____

_____

_____

_____

The Wisdom of Mindset

"Common sense would suggest that having ability, like being smart, inspires confidence. It does, but only while the going is easy. The deciding factor in life is how you handle setbacks and challenges. People with a growth mindset welcome setback with open arms."
-Travis Bradberry

Reflection Time

1. Take a minute to consider yourself and your perception? Are you a fixed mindset person or do you have more of a growth mindset perspective?

_____

_____

_____

_____

2 What steps can I take to be a more open-minded person?

_____

_____

_____

_____

_____

The Wisdom of Self-Care

"Solitude is where I place my chaos to rest and awaken my inner peace."– Nikki Rowe

Reflection Time

1. Are you eating, sleeping and exercising well? Do you feel good in your body or do you feel tired and sluggish? What's working well in this area and what could you improve on?

_____

_____

_____

_____

_____

2. Are you thinking positively, able to access your creativity, and feeling productive? Or are you stressed, getting stuck in negative thoughts, and feeling stuck?

_____

_____

_____

_____

_____

Notes

Notes

Notes

Notes

Notes

Notes

Notes